The Iroquois

by Petra Press

Content Adviser: Professor Sherry L. Field,
Department of Social Science Education, College of Education,
The University of Georgia

Reading Adviser: Dr. Linda D. Labbo,
Department of Reading Education, College of Education,
The University of Georgia

COMPASS POINT BOOKS

Minneapolis, Minnesota

Compass Point Books
3722 West 50th Street, #115
Minneapolis, MN 55410

Visit Compass Point Books on the Internet at *www.compasspointbooks.com* or e-mail your request
to *custserv@compasspointbooks.com*

Photographs ©: McCoy/Visuals Unlimited, cover; Spencer Swanger/Tom Stack and Associates, 4;
Hulton Getty/Archive Photos, 5, 16, 22, 23, 26, 27, 29, 30, 32, 36; Jeff Greenberg/Visuals
Unlimited, 6, 42, 43; XNR Productions, Inc., 7; Stock Montage, 8, 9, 15, 19, 21, 24; North Wind
Picture Archives, 10, 14, 18, 20, 25, 28, 31, 34, 35, 37, 38, 39, 40; Stock Montage/The Newberry
Library, 11, 17; Ken Lucas/Visuals Unlimited, 12; Unicorn Stock Photos/Richard B. Dippold, 13;
Archive Photos, 33; Bruce Gaylord/Visuals Unlimited, 41.

Editors: E. Russell Primm, Emily J. Dolbear, and Alice K. Flanagan
Photo Researcher: Svetlana Zhurkina
Photo Selector: Linda S. Koutris
Designer: Bradfordesign, Inc.

Library of Congress Cataloging-in-Publication Data
Press, Petra.
    The Iroquois / by Petra Press.
       p. cm. — (First reports)
    Includes bibliographical references and index.
    ISBN 0-7565-0080-X (hardcover : lib. bdg.)
    1. Iroquois Indians—History—Juvenile literature. 2. Iroquois Indians—Social life and cus-
toms—Juvenile literature. [1. Iroquois Indians. 2. Indians of North America—New York (State).]
    I. Title. II. Series.
    E99.I7 P74 2001
    974'.0049755—dc21   00-011067

Table of Contents

The Great Iroquois Nation

▲ *The Iroquois lived along the lakes and in the forests of the northern United States and Canada.*

▲ A portrait of an Iroquois warrior

Long before the Europeans arrived, five great Indian tribes lived in the forests of North America. They were called the Mohawk, the Oneida (oh-NY-duh), the Onondaga (ahn-huhn-DAW-guh), the Cayuga (kay-YOO-guh), and the Seneca (she-NIH-kuh).

At first, these tribes were enemies. But by the 1600s, they had joined to form one nation, or **federation**.

In the early 1700s, a sixth group joined them. They were the Tuscarora (thus-kuh-ROHR-uh).

▲ *A young Seneca boy in traditional clothing*

These six nations were called the Iroquois (IHR-uh-kwoy). They called themselves the People of the **Longhouse**. Even today, members of these tribes use this name. The federation is also called the Iroquois League, or the Six Nations.

CANADA

Ontario
Quebec

St. Lawrence

ME.

Lake Superior

Wisconsin

Lake Michigan

Lake Huron

Vt.

N.H.

L. Ontario
New York

Mass.

Michigan

Mississippi

Lake Erie

Iowa

Pennsylvania

R.I.

Conn.

Illinois
Indiana
Ohio

N.J.

UNITED STATES

Md.
Delaware

Mo.

Ohio

W. Va.

Virginia

Chesapeake Bay

Missouri

Kentucky

ATLANTIC OCEAN

Tennessee

North Carolina

South Carolina

0   100 miles
0   100 kilometers

▲ *The original homelands of the Iroquois and their present homes.*

The Iroquois now live near the Great Lakes in Wisconsin, Pennsylvania, and New York. Many also live in Canada, in the provinces of Ontario and Quebec.

People of the Longhouse

▲ *Traditional Iroquois houses*

Winters are cold around the Great Lakes. In the past, the Iroquois built longhouses to live in. They were huge, wooden buildings with round roofs. They looked like giant loaves of bread. Sometimes twelve families lived in each building. They covered the walls and roofs with

▲ Building longhouses

bark from trees. The bark kept the heat from the campfires inside the longhouse.

Each family lived in its own part of the long-house. Family members stored their food and supplies in large baskets. They hung clothing and other items such as tools and weapons on hooks.

There were wooden platforms near the bottom of the walls. They covered them with animal skins. People sat on these platforms during the day and slept on them at night.

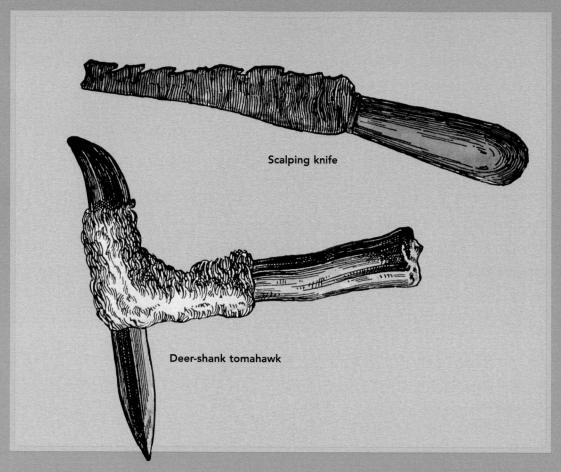

Scalping knife

Deer-shank tomahawk

▲ *Mohawk weapons*

Trees were important to the Iroquois. They used wood to build their houses and to make fires. They made dishes, barrels, tools, weapons, and canoes out of wood. They also built high wooden fences around their villages for safety.

Some people carved wooden masks in living trees and then cut away the masks. Special people called shamans wore the masks to heal the sick.

▲ *A carved wooden ceremonial mask*

Outside the village walls, Iroquois women grew corn, squash, tobacco, and beans. The men fished for bass, pike, and sturgeon. They also hunted for animals. Bear, deer, moose, rabbits, and wild turkeys were among those they hunted most.

▲ *The Iroquois hunted wild turkeys for food.*

▲ *Deer was a staple of the Iroquois diet.*

The Prophet

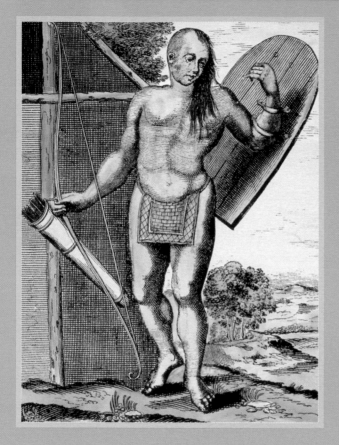

Before the Iroquois nations joined together, they were enemies.

Before the five Iroquois nations formed their federation, they were enemies. They were often at war with one another.

Then one day, a leader from the Huron Indians went from tribe to tribe to talk to people. His name was Deganawida. Some people called him the Prophet. Deganawida wanted peace. He told the tribes they would be stronger if they all got along with one another. He asked them to live together in the shade of a "Great Tree of Peace."

Deganawida said there were thirteen laws the people should follow. If they followed these laws, they would have peace. And they would become the largest Indian nation.

▲ *A council of Indian leaders*

The tribes liked Deganawida's ideas. They agreed to form a new government. The longhouse was chosen as the symbol of the new government.

▲ *Chief Hiawatha helped bring peace to his people.*

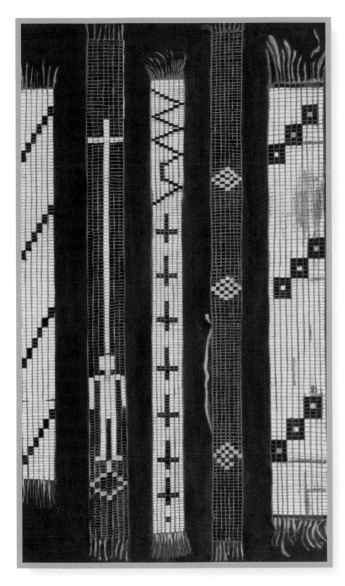
▲ *Wampum belts*

Deganawida and his friend Hiawatha recorded the laws of the new government on a belt made of colored beads. With the beads, they formed designs and symbols. Each of these designs and symbols had special meanings. The Iroquois called those beads **wampum**. They recorded treaties and important events on wampum. All together, the wampum are a history of the Iroquois people.

Clans and Councils

Every Iroquois family belonged to a larger group of relatives. The larger groups were called **clans**. All the families who lived together in a longhouse belonged to the same clan.

The clans had animal names. These names included Turtle, Bear, and Wolf. The spirits of these animals protected the lives of the members of the clan.

A clan mother headed each clan. She owned most of the property. She passed on her family name to her children. When children grew up and married, the couple came to live with the wife's family.

▲ *Symbols of the Iroquois clans*

▲ *Women made great contributions to Iroquois life.*

The families of each longhouse chose the clan mother. The clan mothers chose the members of the **tribal council**. And the tribal council chose the members of the Grand Council.

▲ *An Iroquois tribal council*

The Grand Council met in late summer or early fall at Onondaga. Onondaga was the center of the Iroquois federation. The council made sure everyone followed the laws of the federation.

Every Iroquois had a say in how the government was run. Every person had a vote. It was a democracy. The people called their government the Great Law of the Iroquois League.

Iroquois Religion

Religion was an important part of Iroquois life. Both men and women were chosen to be Keepers of the Faith. The keepers were in charge of religious ceremonies. They healed the sick. They held celebrations every year to thank the creator for good harvests. Often they held ceremonies to honor treaties made with other tribes.

▲ *Iroquois dance to honor the Great Spirit.*

The Iroquois believed that all life was important. Everything in the world had a spirit of its own. A person who wanted to be happy in life had to keep the spirits happy.

The Iroquois have many beautiful myths and legends. One explains why Earth is carried around on the back of a giant turtle.

▲ *All life, human and animal, is sacred to the Iroquois.*

Rise to Power

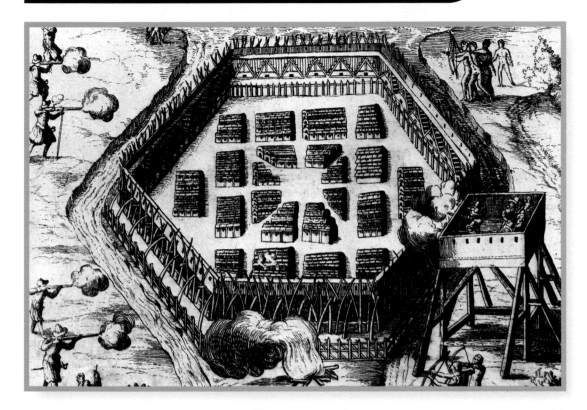

▲ *The combined Iroquois nations were very powerful.*

After the Iroquois formed the federation, the tribes got along with one another. But they continued to fight their enemies. The Iroquois wanted larger hunting grounds. They fought many wars with other tribes to get more land.

▲ *As settlers came to Iroquois lands, the chiefs had to deal with problems such as disease.*

By the 1600s, the Iroquois federation was very powerful. It was the strongest Indian nation north of Mexico.

In the mid-1600s, the Iroquois began dying of an illness called smallpox. White trappers and settlers had brought the disease with them from Europe. By 1650, half of the Iroquois people had died of smallpox or in wars.

▲ The Iroquois adopted their prisoners of war.

The Iroquois found a way to increase their population. They no longer killed their prisoners of war. Instead, they adopted them! They brought their prisoners into their longhouses to live. They made them members of clans.

The Iroquois brought many new people into the federation this way. Soon, the Iroquois Confederacy was strong again.

The Fur Trade

In the 1600s, French and English trappers began hunting in Iroquois country. They came to trap beaver. At that time, people in Europe were paying high prices for hats and coats made of beaver fur.

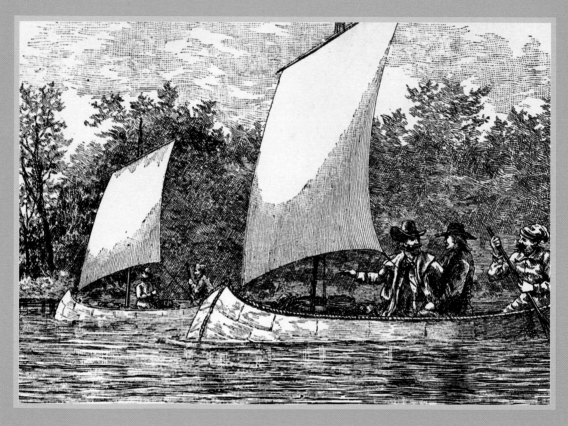

▲ *French and English fur traders entered Iroquois lands in the 1600s.*

▲ *Europeans built forts to protect themselves from angry American Indians.*

The trappers sold the furs to traders. Then the traders shipped the furs to Europe. The beaver trade was a big business. Soon the traders built forts.

▲ *Iroquois began trapping beavers to trade for other goods.*

Before long, the Iroquois saw that trapping beavers for the traders was a good idea. The traders had many things the Iroquois wanted. They could trade beaver pelts for coffee, tools, blankets, beads, and guns.

By 1650, the Iroquois had trapped most of the fur-bearing animals in their homeland. They began to look for new hunting grounds. They went to lands claimed by the Huron and other Great Lakes tribes.

Soon, the Iroquois were fighting wars over the fur trade. They were called the Beaver Wars. The wars lasted from the late 1670s until 1701.

▲ *The Iroquois began to move into the lands of nearby nations.*

▲ *French explorer Samuel de Champlain attacks an Iroquois settlement.*

At first, only the Iroquois and the western Indian tribes fought in the wars. But soon the French started to help the western tribes fight the Iroquois. The Iroquois then made friends with the British **colonists**. The French and the British were longtime enemies. The British helped the Iroquois fight the French.

That war lasted from 1754 to 1763. It is called the French and Indian War. In the end, the British and the Iroquois won. Over the next several years, the British colonists began thinking of themselves as Americans.

▲ *The Iroquois joined forces with the British to fight the French.*

The American Revolution

By 1775, many of the American colonists wanted to be free from Britain. They wanted to set up a country of their own. They started a war with Britain. It is called the American **Revolution**.

In the past, the Iroquois fought with the British against the French. Now some of the Iroquois did not think it was such

▲ *Mohawk chief Joseph Brant (above) and Seneca chief Cornplanter (right) supported the British*

a good idea to fight alongside the British. The confederation split in half. Most Iroquois fought with the
British. But some fought with the colonists.

General George Washington led the American army. In May 1779, he ordered his troops to destroy the Iroquois villages. They burned eleven towns with about 165 log homes. They destroyed more than 500 acres (202 hectares) of land. They killed and captured thousands of people. Many Iroquois fled to Canada, where their families still live today.

▲ U.S. troops were ordered to destroy Indian villages.

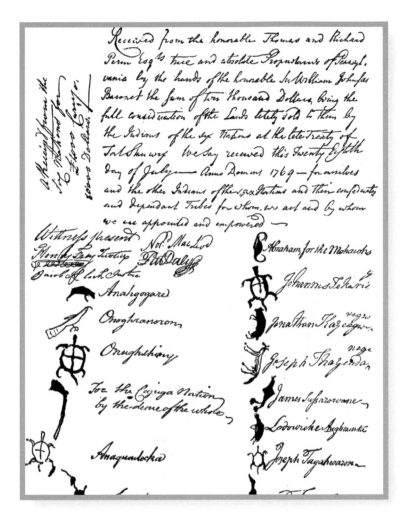

▲ An Indian deed

In 1783, the American colonists won the American Revolution. They formed the United States of America. The new government was run a lot like the Iroquois federation.

Reservation Life

▲ *A Mohawk village after the American Revolution*

After the American Revolution, the Iroquois confederation was over. The Indians had lost their homeland. Most of the land they once lived on

▲ *The Iroquois tried to continue their traditions on the reservation.*

was given or sold to white settlers. Only a small part of it became a **reservation** for the Six Nations. A reservation is land that the U.S. government sets aside for Indian tribes to live on.

Life was hard on the reservation for the Iroquois. Often, the Indians had to sell their land to white settlers to buy food. In some cases, white settlers stole their land.

In 1830, the U.S. government forced the Iroquois to move to new reservations in the Midwest. Thousands of people had to move to parts of Kansas, Wisconsin, and southern Canada. In 1867, the Indians living in Kansas were forced to move again—this time to Oklahoma. Twenty years later, they had to move yet again.

▲ *Thousands of Iroquois moved west in the 1830s.*

▲ *Reservation life was difficult.*

On the reservation, people lacked food, clothing, blankets, and tools. Many people died. The adults were not allowed to speak their own language. They were not allowed to practice their religion. The U.S. government sent their children away to **boarding schools.** At these boarding schools, the children had to live like white Americans. They were taught a new language and a new way to dress.

Modern Iroquois

▲ *The Iroquois adopted traditional farming ways.*

In the late 1920s, reservation life began to improve. The government spent more money on schools and hospitals. Native Americans were allowed to become citizens of the United States. But through all the hard

▲ *A modern Mohawk in traditional dress*

times, the Iroquois held on to their religion and their beliefs. They kept their traditions alive. The Iroquois still hold council meetings. They celebrate many of the old ceremonies.

Today, the Iroquois people are citizens of the
United States or Canada. But they are also members
of the Iroquois Nation. In 1989, the Onondaga
Indians got back twelve of their traditional wampum
belts from the state of New York. Once again, they
are the wampum keepers of the Iroquois League.

▲ *Iroquois are U.S. or Canadian citizens*
as well as members of the Iroquois nation.

▲ *Iroquois traditions are passed from generation to generation.*

Today, the Iroquois work at all kinds of jobs. Some are doctors, lawyers, and teachers. Some people raise cattle and some grow fruit. Others are artists, writers, and musicians. Many work in the tourist trade or in the casinos.

No matter where they are or what they do, the Iroquois have never forgotten who they are. They still are, and always will be, Haudenosaunee—the People of the Longhouse.

Glossary

boarding schools—schools where students live

clans—groups of related families

colonists—people who live in a newly settled area

federation—a union of nations

longhouse—a large wooden building with a barrel-shaped roof

reservation—a large area of land set aside for Native Americans; in Canada, reservations are called reserves

revolution—a war fought to change the government

tribal council—a group of people who make laws or rules for a tribe

wampum—small beads strung together in designs to record events; sometimes used as money

Did You Know?

- Benjamin Franklin and Thomas Jefferson took many of their ideas about democracy and equal rights from the Iroquois League.

- Iroquois men and women decorated their bodies with tattoos.

- Some Iroquois wore wooden masks to scare off evil spirits that caused illness. The group was called the False Face Society.

- The Iroquois invented a ball game called lacrosse. Players use a long-handled stick with a mesh pouch to catch, carry, and throw the ball.

At a Glance

Tribal name: Iroquois

Divisions: Mohawk, Oneida, Onondaga, Cayuga, Seneca, Tuscarora

Past locations: New York, Pennsylvania, Ohio, Indiana, Wisconsin, Kansas, Oklahoma; Ontario and Quebec in Canada

Present locations: Wisconsin, New York, Pennsylvania; Ontario and Quebec in Canada

Traditional houses: Longhouses

Traditional clothing material: Skins, feathers, fibers

Traditional transportation: Elm-bark and birch-bark canoes, snowshoes

Traditional food: Corn, meat, fish, wild plants

Important Dates

1570–1600	The prophet Deganawida spreads a message of peace; the Iroquois League is formed.
1650	War and disease kill half of the Iroquois people.
late 1670s–1701	The Iroquois fight against western tribes in the Beaver Wars.
1776–1783	Most Iroquois fight on the British side during the American Revolution.
1779	General George Washington's troops destroy Iroquois villages; Iroquois people are forced off most of their land.
1830	The U.S. government forces the Iroquois to move to new reservations in the Midwest.
1867	The Iroquois in Kansas are moved to a reservation in Oklahoma.
1870–1920	The Iroquois are not allowed to speak their own language or follow their old traditions; the U.S. government sends Iroquois children to boarding schools.
1989	Onondaga Indians get back twelve of their traditional wampum belts from New York; once again, they are the wampum keepers of the Iroquois League.

Want to Know More?

At the Library

Bruchac, Joseph. *Children of the Longhouse*. New York: Dial Books for Young Readers, 1996.

Driving Hawk Sneve, Virginia. *The Iroquois*. New York: Holiday House, 1995.

McCall, Barbara A. *The Iroquois*. Vero Beach, Fla.: Rourke Publishing Group, 1990.

Ridington, Jillian, and Robin Ridington. *People of the Longhouse: How the Iroquoian Tribes Lived*. Toronto: Firefly Books, 1995.

On the Web

Iroquois Confederacy Links
http://www.axess.com/mohawk/links_misc.htm
For information on the Iroquois Confederacy

Haudenosaunee Iroquois Homework Help
http://www.peace4turtleisland.org/pages/homework.htm
For information for students about the Iroquois

Through the Mail

The Oneida Indian Nation
223 Genesee Street
Oneida, NY 13421
To write for information about the Oneida culture and history

On the Road

The Seneca-Iroquois National Museum
794 Broad Street
Salamanca, NY 14779
716/945-1738
To see exhibits about the prehistoric, historic, and contemporary life of the Seneca and Iroquois people

Index

About the Author

Petra Press is a freelance writer of young adult nonfiction, specializing in the diverse culture of the Americas. Her more than twenty books include histories of U.S. immigration, education, and settlement of the West, as well as portraits of numerous indigenous cultures. She lives in Milwaukee, Wisconsin, with her husband, David.